Chocolate & Banana

THE SEXIEST OF CLASSICS

LINDA SAUVÉ

Copyright © Linda Sauvé 2013

All rights reserved. No part of this publication may be reproduced or transmitted in any form or by any means, electronic or mechanical, including photocopying, recording, or any other information storage and retrieval system, without the written permission of the author.

Photo credit: Marc van Eyken
Photo assistant: Elisabeth van Eyken and Evelyn van Eyken
Food stylist: Linda Sauvé
Edited: Danielle Hards and Linda Sauvé
Cover design: Catherine McDonnell
Interior design: Stephanie Anderson, Jera Publishing

eISBN 978-2-9814126-2-1
ISBN (print) 978-2-9814126-3-8

Catalogue: Chocolate, Food & Drink, Baking and Desserts,

To contact the author, please use the following coordinates.

220 Kenyon Street West, Unit 207
Alexandria, Ontario K0C 1A0
organisemoi@hotmail.com

Visit www.organisemoi.ca

Dedicated to all those

who cannot live without

this dream pair.

From the same author

French publications

Organise-moi ça! 1ère édition chez Tremplin en 2005, réédition augmentée en 2006 aux Éditions Goélette, réédition en 2010 chez Les éditions Coup d'œil. 265 pages.

Cinq minutes pour faire une scène, Édition Tam-Tam, 2006, 156 pages.

Comment faire? – 50 experts répondent à 1001 questions qui vous chicotent – Les Éditions Transcontinental, 2009, 278 pages.

All publications are available on the author's web site at
www.organisemoi.ca

Contents

Breakfast

Chocolate and banana energizing pollen smoothie 7

Chocolate and banana gourmet grilled cheese 9

Banana and coconut pancakes with
chocolate and maple syrup sauce 10

Chocolate and banana strata 13

Chocolate and banana kugel-cloud 15

Chocolate and banana protein bar 17

Sweet burger. 18

Banana sauce 19

Chocolate spread 19

Muffin in a jar. 21

Snacks

Chocolate and banana praline cylinder 25

Chocolate and banana lava cake 27

Banana and chocolate ice cream 29

No guilty pleasure cookies 31

Chocolate and banana Madeleine 33

Chocolate, rice and banana chips bark. 35

Sexy surprise chocolate banana donut holes 37

Dessert

White chocolate and banana meringue tarts 41
Brazilia 43
7th heaven chocolate and banana pie 45
Unordinary chocolate and banana bread 47
Chocolate and banana royal cake 49
Incredible raw chocolate banana brownies 51
Chocolate and caramelized bananas empanadas 53

Beauty

Chocolate and banana scrub 57
Chocolate and banana body butter 59
Chocolate bath bombs 61

Introduction

CHOCOLATE AND BANANA are always a winning combination whether served at breakfast, as a snack or as a dessert. Plates are emptied quickly to the chief's delight.

Why choose this twosome to write a cookbook? Just because I LOVE dishes prepared with these ingredients. They are alkalizing, filled with goodness and healthy.

BLACK CHOCOLATE[*]: antioxidants (anti-rust for the arteries), magnesium (natural anti-anxiety mineral), flavonoids (antioxidant and anti-inflammatory properties with a potential protective effect of the heart and the brain), phenylethylamine or PEA (acts as an antidepressant: a substance that the body produces when we are in love), theobromine (a natural energy molecule that is caffeine-free and provides a feeling of well-being).

BANANA: potassium (calming effect), magnesium, iron, manganese, tryptophan (that the body converts into serotonin), vitamin C (primary antioxidant) vitamin B6 (regulates hormones such as estrogen and progesterone and decreases symptoms of PMS), and fibre-rich carbohydrates (facilitate recovery after exercise).

---

[*] For chocolate to be considered black the following must be true: the first ingredient listed must be chocolate or cocoa butter, there must be an expiry date on the package, and contain a cocoa percentage of 70% or more. If the first ingredient in the list is sugar, it is not black chocolate.

These vitamins and minerals won't replace your daily multi-vitamin, but they will support your body and mind during your activities and may well put an enigmatic smile on your face.

In order to gather all my favorite recipes in a book, I searched my own recipes and recipes from other cultures fond of this dream duo. I created, adapted and revisited all recipes selected for the sole pleasure of tasting them again and again.

You will discover that you can enjoy these classics from morning to evening and can stretch the indulgence by coating your body with them or linger in an aromatic bath. Enjoy!

Linda Sauvé
CHOCOHOLIC

** cover photo shows the Chocolate and Banana praline cylinder.

GLUTEN FREE RECIPE OPTIONS

All recipes requiring flour can be prepared with gluten-free flour composed of three-quarter cup of buckwheat flour and ¼ cup of rice flour if the required quantity is one cup, unless stated otherwise.

We recommend that you sift the buckwheat flour twice to remove the blackish bark of the grounded grain. Do not pack the flour. Putting a pan of water in a corner of the oven while baking gluten-free recipes will prevent drying.

LACTOSE FREE RECIPE OPTIONS

When dairy products are required in a recipe, they can be replaced by their lactose free equivalent: soy milk for cow's milk, soy cream for 15% cream, goat yogurt for sour cream. The whipping cream in the Brazilia does not have a substitute.

TABLE OF CONVERSION

°C	°F	Thermostat
100	200	3
120	250	4
150	300	5
180	350	6
200	400	7
230	450	8
260	500	9
BROIL	GRIL	

SPICES WHICH PAIR WELL WITH THE BANANA

French 4 spices mixture: 1 tsp. (5 ml) nutmeg, 1 tsp. (5 ml) Jamaican pepper, ¼ tsp. (2 ml) English clove and 1 tsp. (5 ml) ginger.

SPICES WHICH PAIR WELL WITH BLACK CHOCOLATE

Cardamom, chili flakes, cinnamon, sea salt, fleur de sel, orange and lemon zest.

FRUITS WHICH PAIR WELL WITH BLACK CHOCOLATE BESIDES BANANA

Clementine, pear, cantaloupe, mango, apple and strawberry.

Breakfast

Chocolate and banana energizing pollen smoothie 7

Chocolate and banana gourmet grilled cheese 9

Banana and coconut pancakes with
chocolate and maple syrup sauce 10

Chocolate and banana strata 13

Chocolate and banana kugel-cloud 15

Chocolate and banana protein bar 17

Sweet burger 18
Banana sauce. 19
Chocolate spread 19

Muffin in a jar 21

BREAKFAST

Chocolate and banana energizing pollen smoothie

Pollen is a complete food. It contains 185 nutrients including: 22 amino acids, 27 essential minerals such as calcium, iodine, iron, magnesium, manganese, potassium, selenium, zinc and a wide spectrum of vitamins especially the antioxidants such as vitamins A, C and E and is a good source of vitamin B12. Finally, pollen has more protein (35% by weight) than most foods deemed rich in proteins. Keep your pollen in the refrigerator to preserve all of its properties. Buy it locally from your honey producer.

Servings:
One portion

Ingredients:
1 to 2 Tbsp. (15 to 30 ml) fresh pollen

½ frozen banana, cut into small slices

1 Tbsp. (15 ml) cocoa powder

1 Tbsp. (15 ml) honey

1 handful cashews

1 cup (250 ml) milk

Directions:
1. Mix all ingredients in a blender. Serve immediately.
2. Pollen will tend to stay at the bottom of the glass, stir occasionally while drinking.

Chef's Note:
Peel and slice your bananas before you freeze them.

BREAKFAST

Chocolate and banana gourmet grilled cheese

Servings:
4 grilled cheese

Ingredients:
2 mashed bananas (½ banana per portion)

8 slices of bread (rice bread, challah, ciabatta or coconut pancakes found on the next page) about half-inch thick

Soft butter

¼ cup (60 ml) semi-sweet chocolate chips

8 oz. of Brie cheese (cow or goat cheese) cut into thin slices

Directions:

1. Butter one side of each of the 8 slices of bread.
2. Place 4 slices of bread butter-side-down onto skillet.
3. Evenly divide and spread the mashed bananas on the 4 slices of bread in the skillet. Garnish with chocolate chips then add the Brie.
4. Place the remaining bread butter-side-up on top of sandwich.
5. Cook 4 to 7 minutes on each side over a medium heat until they turn brown.
6. Slightly press the grilled cheese with a spatula before you turn them.
7. Remove from the skillet. Let rest a minute and then serve.

Banana and coconut pancakes with chocolate and maple syrup sauce

BREAKFAST

Servings:
14 pancakes

Ingredients:

½ cup (125 ml) rolled oats or quinoa (depending on your tolerance)

½ cup (125 ml) unsweetened coconut

1 cup (250 ml) sifted flour

¼ cup (60 ml) brown sugar (optional)

1 tsp. (5 ml) baking powder

1 tsp. (5 ml) baking soda

A pinch of salt

A pinch of nutmeg powder

1 ripe banana

2 beaten eggs

1 cup (250 ml) plain yogurt

½ cup (125 ml) milk

2 Tbsp. (30 ml) vegetable oil for cooking

Maple syrup flavoured with cocoa liquor for topping on pancakes.

Directions:

1. In a large bowl, combine the first 8 ingredients.
2. In another bowl, mash the banana then add the eggs and the yogurt. Whisk together.
3. Stir in the milk. Add the wet mixture to the dry mixture.
4. Mix until uniform consistency.
5. Pour the vegetable oil into a large skillet over a medium heat. When the skillet is hot, pour ¼ cup (60 ml) of dough per pancake.
6. Spread the dough slightly. Do not cramp too many pancakes in a skillet. Cook until bubbles form on the surface, about 2 or 3 minutes, then gently flip them over and cook for another 2 minutes.
7. Cook until pancakes are golden on both sides.
8. Serve with cocoa liqueur flavored maple syrup.

SYRUP: Add 6 ml of cocoa liquor per 125 ml of maple syrup or other table syrup. Another recipe of chocolate syrup is also available in the Chocolate and banana royal cake recipe.

Chef's note:

Lower the heat to low to avoid burning the oil. Increase the amount of liquor according to the taste.

BREAKFAST

Chocolate and banana strata

Servings:
4 to 8 servings

Ingredients:
4 slice of bread

4 eggs

1 cup (250 ml) milk

1 cup (250 ml) banana cut into slices (about one large banana)

¼ cup (60 ml) chocolate chips

Directions:

1. Preheat oven to 325 °F or 160 °C.
2. Cut the bread into 2 inch (1 cm) cubes.
3. Whisk the eggs and the milk in a medium bowl and add the rest of the ingredients.
4. Blend with a large spoon.
5. Pour evenly in 4 ramekins of 8 oz. (1 cup) or 8 ramekins of 4 oz. (½ cup) and place on a baking sheet.
6. Bake for 35 minutes for the large ramequins and 30 minutes for the smaller ones or until the preparation is puffed and top is set.
7. Serve warm.

OPTIONS: A muffin pan can easily replace the ramekins. Chocolate bread can also be used. In this instance, reduce the quantity of chocolate chips to 2 Tbsp. (30 ml).

BREAKFAST

Chocolate and banana kugel-cloud

The kugel is a traditional Jewish dish that is served during certain holidays. Chocolate and banana mixed with the classical Kugel can be hard to digest, but my adaptation will feel like a cloud in your mouth. It will soon become your go-to dish for breakfast or dessert because it is low in sugar and fat.

Servings:
8 servings

Ingredients:
180 g pound cake

½ cup (125 ml) hot water

½ cup (125 ml) cream of cocoa (an alcohol made from cocoa)

1 cup (250 ml) mashed bananas (2 medium or one large one)

3 Tbsp. (45 ml) black chocolate chips (70% cocoa)

3 egg whites beaten stiff

1 ¼ tsp. (6 ml) ground cinnamon

Directions:

1. Preheat oven to 350 °F or 180 °C.
2. Grease a square 8-inch pan or a 2 liter pan.
3. Cut the pound cake into 1 inch or 2.5 cm cubes and reserve.
4. Mash the bananas.
5. In a small saucepan, combine the water and the alcohol and heat until warm.
6. Wait for the oven to be ready before beating egg whites to a stiff consistency in a cold bowl.
7. Coat the cake cubes with the mixture of water and alcohol.
8. Add the bananas and the chocolate chips and then fold in the stiff egg whites into the mixture. Pour into prepared pan. Sprinkle the kugel-cloud evenly with the cinnamon.
9. Place in the oven immediately.
10. Cook for 45 minutes. Serve warm.

BREAKFAST

Chocolate and banana protein bar

Servings:
8 bars

Ingredients:
3 large eggs

½ cup (125 ml) milk

1 Tbsp. (15 ml) vegetable oil

1 ¼ cup (300 ml) mashed bananas, about 3 medium bananas

1 tsp. (5 ml) ground cinnamon

2 Tbsp. (30 ml) cocoa powder unsweetened

¾ cup (180 ml) rolled oats

⅓ cup (80 ml) sugar

¼ cup (60 ml) meal replacement protein powder

Directions:

1. Preheat oven to 350° F or 180° C.
2. In a large bowl, beat the eggs then add the milk, oil and bananas and mix well.
3. Add the remaining ingredients. Mix until well combined.
4. Pour the mixture into a square greased pan (8 x 8 or 2 liter pan).
5. Bake for 50 minutes or until firm.
6. Allow to cool completely before cutting into 8 pieces.

Gives about 5 g of protein per bar. For even more protein, add half cup (125 ml) of slivered almonds.

These bars remain soft even at room temperature.

BREAKFAST

Sweet burger

Directions:

1. Get a bag of store bought vanilla cookies preferably round and soft.

2. Brush chocolate spread on the inside of a cookie, add a teaspoon of banana sauce and top with a second cookie.

3. Makes a quick lunch on the go (it is full of protein, fiber and vitamins).

This sweet burger can easily be prepared for a kid's party.

ANOTHER SWEET BURGER OPTION: use soft store bought chocolate cookies to prepare a frozen sandwich made with the banana and chocolate ice cream found in this cookbook.

Try the two recipes on the following page on a sweet burger.

Banana sauce

Ingredients:

2 mashed bananas

½ tsp. (2 ml or less depending on your preference) cardamom or 4 spices mixture

Zest of one lemon and its juice (approximately 2 Tbsp. (30 ml) of juice)

¼ cup (60 ml) maple syrup or brown sugar

Directions:

1 Heat the maple syrup or brown sugar until it bubbles and caramelizes.

2 Add the bananas, lemon zest, lemon juice, the spices and cook for 2 minutes.

3 Serve warm or cold.

Chocolate spread

Ingredients:

1 cup (250 ml) pitted dates cooked in a little water and cooled.

½ cup (125 ml) almond butter

½ cup (125 ml) cocoa powder

Vanilla to taste

Directions:

1 Put all ingredients in a food processor and pulse until smooth.

2 Will keep in the refrigerator up to a week (if you can resist!).

Chef's note:

Try another nut butter such as hazelnut butter to replace the almond butter.

BREAKFAST

Muffin in a jar

Servings:
6 muffins

Ingredients:

DRY INGREDIENTS

1 cup (250 ml) flour

1½ tsp. (7 ml) baking powder

½ tsp. (2 ml) baking soda

2 Tbsp. (30 ml) sugar

2 tsp. (10 ml) cocoa powder

¼ cup (60 ml) semi-sweet chocolate chips

WET INGREDIENTS

2 Tbsp. (30 ml) olive oil

¾ cup (180 ml) milk

1 medium banana, mashed

1 beaten egg

Directions:

1. Preheat oven to 350° F or 180° C.
2. Mix the dry ingredients in a bowl. Mix the wet ingredients in another bowl.
3. Add the wet mixture into the dry mixture.
4. Stir only until just combined otherwise the dough will harden.
5. Pour mixture into a greased muffin pan.
6. Bake for 20 minutes.

Gift Idea:

Write or print the recipe on a pretty card or paper and put all dry ingredients in a Mason jar. Add a bow or ribbon.

Snacks

Chocolate and banana praline cylinder 25

Chocolate and banana lava cake 27

Banana and chocolate ice cream 29

No guilty pleasure cookies 31

Chocolate and banana Madeleine 33

Chocolate, rice and banana chips bark. 35

Sexy surprise chocolate banana donut holes 37

SNACKS

Chocolate and banana praline cylinder

Servings:
12 cylinders

Ingredients:
6 bananas, peeled

1 cup (250 ml) melted black chocolate chips (70% cocoa)

½ cup (125 ml) roasted slivered almonds

Directions:

1. Peel and cut bananas in half.
2. Dip and coat one end of each cylinder of bananas with melted black chocolate
3. Then coat the cylinders with slivered almonds.
4. Put in cocktail glasses and allow to cool vertically (as shown in photo) in the fridge.

Serve as a snack or with a pound cake and whipped cream for a sexy dessert.

SNACKS

Chocolate and banana lava cake

Servings:
8 servings

Ingredients:
7 oz. (200 ml) black chocolate

⅔ cup (160 ml) 5% cream (you can also use 10% cream if you desire)

3 eggs, separated

½ cup (125 ml) sugar

⅓ cup (80 ml) flour

1 ½ ripe bananas

Directions:
1. Preheat oven to 350 °F or 180 °C.
2. Melt the chocolate in a double boiler with cream.
3. Beat the yolks and sugar until creamy.
4. Add the cream and chocolate mixture to egg yolks and then add the flour with a spatula. Beat the egg whites until stiff.
5. Fold the egg whites into the chocolate mixture.
6. Pour half of the dough into a square or rectangular Pyrex buttered pan, add fairly thick slices of bananas on top of the mixture and then pour the rest of the mixture.
7. Bake on the middle rack for 25 minutes.
8. Allow to cool for 15 minutes then cut into squares.
9. If the squares are too runny, wait a little longer before serving.

To make this recipe gluten-free and lactose-free, use cream of soybean and millet and rice flours.

SNACKS

Banana and chocolate ice cream

Servings:
4 servings

Ingredients:
1 ¼ cup (300 ml) frozen bananas, sliced (about 2 large ones)

2 Tbsp. (30 ml) cocoa powder

Juice of half a lemon (about 1 Tbsp.)

2 egg whites

Directions:
1. Place all ingredients in a food processor.
2. Blend for about 30 seconds until smooth consistency is achieved.
3. Transfer to a freezer safe plastic container.
4. Store in the freezer without delay.

PRESENTATION OPTION: Serve with dry cookies or chocolate pizzelle.

SNACKS

No guilty pleasure cookies

Servings:

24 cookies

Ingredients:

1 ½ cup (375 ml) pitted dates

½ medium banana, mashed

2 Tbsp. (30 ml) sunflower or canola oil

A few drops of vanilla

2 beaten eggs

¾ cup (180 ml) flour

½ cup (125 ml) black chocolate chips 70% cocoa

2 Tbsp. (30 ml) cocoa powder

1 ½ tsp. (7 ml) baking powder

A Pinch of ground cinnamon

A Pinch of salt

Directions:

1. In a large bowl, cover dates with hot water. Allow to cool for 30 minutes. Drain excess water. Reserve.
2. Preheat oven to 350° F or 180° C.
3. Position the oven rack in the center of the oven.
4. Line one or two cookie sheets with parchment paper.
5. Add the banana, oil, and vanilla to the cooled dates. Mix well then add the eggs.
6. Mix all dry ingredients, including the chocolate chips, in a bowl.
7. Add the dry ingredients to the wet mixture and mix.
8. Drop one spoonful per cookie onto the cookie sheets and bake for about 14 minutes.
9. The cookies will have the appearance of not being cooked and that is normal.
10. Cool on a rack and store in an airtight container in the refrigerator.

Serving them warm will make the tasting experience even sexier.

SNACKS

Chocolate and banana Madeleines

Servings:
24 madeleines

Ingredients:

⅓ cup (80 ml) unsalted butter

½ cup (125 ml) flour

1 tsp. (5 ml) baking powder

2 eggs

⅓ cup (80 ml) sugar

4 Tbsp. (60 ml) milk

A pinch of salt

½ banana mashed

2 Tbsp. (30 ml) black or white chocolate chips

1 Tbsp. (15 ml) cocoa powder or icing sugar

2 madeleine pans.

Directions:

1. Preheat oven to 450 °F or 230 °C.
2. Melt the butter on low heat in a saucepan or in the microwave, then leave to cool.
3. Sift the flour and the baking powder twice. (It makes a better batter.)
4. Beat the eggs and sugar until smooth, and then add the milk and salt.
5. Add the mixture of flour and baking powder to the egg mixture.
6. Add the melted butter and the banana, and then add the chocolate chips.
7. Butter and flour madeleine pans.
8. Using two spoons, fill each madeleine cell up to ⅔ capacity.
9. Cook for 5 minutes at 450° F or 230° C and then lower the temperature to 375° F or 190° C and cook for another 5 minutes.
10. Remove from pan immediately, let cool on a wired rack and sprinkle cocoa powder or icing sugar over the ribbed side.

Chef's note:

The madeleine will keep in the refrigerator for up to 10 days in an airtight container.

SNACKS

Chocolate, rice and banana chips bark

Servings:
5 servings

Ingredients:
1 ½ cup (375 ml) black chocolate chips 70%

½ cup (125 ml) Rice Krispies cereals

½ cup (125 ml) bananas chips (no salt or seasoning) crushed by hand

¼ cup (60 ml) natural almonds crushed coarsely (optional)

Directions:
1. Line pan with parchment paper, leaving 1 inch (2.5 cm) overhang on long sides.

2. Melt the chocolate in a double boiler over low heat, stirring often, until almost melted. Do not overheat. Remove from heat. Stir until smooth.

3. Add the remaining ingredients.

4. Pour on prepared pan and spread using a silicone spatula.

5. Chill for about an hour until set. Remove from pan. Break bark into irregular-shaped pieces and enjoy.

6. Freeze up to three weeks, lined with the parchment paper in an airtight bag or container. Packed in decorative tin, this bark makes a delicious gift.

OPTION: Melt a ½ cup (125 g) of white chocolate in the microwave at medium power for a few seconds then drizzle over the bark before breaking into irregular-shaped pieces, about 1 ½ x 4 inches (3.8 x 10 cm) each.

SNACKS

Sexy surprise chocolate banana donut holes

Servings:
24 donuts

Ingredients:
3 bananas (medium size, ripe but still firm)

Two inches of oil in a small heavy-bottomed saucepan

FOR THE BATTER:

Its consistency will be that of a pancake batter

½ cup (125 ml) flour

¼ tsp. (1 ml) baking powder

A pinch of salt

1 beaten egg

⅓ cup (80 ml) water or a little more depending on consistency

Cocoa powder or melted chocolate for presentation

Directions:

1. Peel the bananas and cut them into 8 pieces.
2. Mix all ingredients for the batter and whisk until smooth.
3. Heat the oil over a medium heat.
4. With a fork, dip each piece of banana in the batter.
5. Coat evenly, then drop it slowly with the help of another fork in the hot oil and fry for about 5 minutes.
6. Turn them at the halfway point. Fry until they are evenly browned.
7. Drain on paper towels.
8. Sprinkle with cocoa powder while they are still hot or dip them in the melted chocolate and then allow to cool on a rack.

Dessert

White chocolate and banana meringue tarts 41

Brazilia 43

7th heaven chocolate and banana pie 45

Unordinary chocolate and banana bread 47

Chocolate and banana royal cake 49

Incredible raw chocolate banana brownies 51

Chocolate and caramelized bananas empanadas 53

White chocolate and banana meringue tarts

DESSERT

Ingredients:

2 thawed store bought pie crusts

1 ½ cup (375 ml) milk

½ cup (125 ml) sugar

⅓ cup (80 ml) corn starch

1 cup (250 ml) white chocolate chips

Finely chopped zest of one lemon

½ ripe banana mashed

⅓ cup (80 ml) homemade banana liqueur

2 Tbsp. (30 ml) butter cut into cubes

HOMEMADE BANANA LIQUEUR

1 Tbsp. (15 ml) water

1 Tbsp. (15 ml) sugar

2 Tbsp. (30 ml) vodka

3 drops of artificial essence of banana

MERINGUE

4 egg whites at room temperature

½ tsp. (2.5 ml) cream of tartar

⅓ cup (80 ml) sugar

Servings: 20 tarts

Directions:

1. Preheat oven to 400 °F or 200 °C.
2. Place cupcake liners in two muffin pans.
3. Cut the dough into 3 ½ inches (9 cm) rounds using a ramekin as a cutter.
4. Lay the dough in cupcake liners.
5. Bake in the oven for 12 minutes or according to the manufacturer's instructions and then allow to cool completely.
6. Meanwhile, whisk the milk with cornstarch and sugar in a heavy-bottomed saucepan over medium heat.
7. Cook, stirring constantly, until the mixture becomes very thick, remove from the heat. Stir in white chocolate chips and whisk until they are melted.
8. Add banana liqueur, mashed banana and lemon zest and whisk until smooth.
9. Gradually stir in the butter until it is completely incorporated to the mixture.
10. Pour this filling into the cooled crust.

MERINGUE

1. Adjust the oven to 325° F or 160° C
2. Beat egg whites and cream of tartar with an electric mixer at high speed until foamy. Beating constantly, gradually add the sugar and whisk until the firm peaks.
3. Add the meringue to the tarts making sure to smooth it up to the edge of the crust.
4. Bake 15 to 18 minutes or until golden.
5. Cool to room temperature.
6. Refrigerate for at least 2 hours before serving.

Will stay fresh for a few days in the refrigerator in an airtight container.

DESSERT

Brazilia

Servings:
6 portions

Ingredients:
1 cup (250 ml) chocolate cookies, crumbled

4 large bananas

2 Tbsp. (30 ml) lime juice

4 Tbsp. (60 ml) melted butter

⅓ cup (80 ml) icing sugar

1 egg

1 Tbsp. (15 ml) strong coffee

1 ¼ cup (300 ml) whipped cream

1 banana, sliced

2 tsp. (10 ml) lime juice

Directions:

1. Spread half of the cookie crumbs in a 8 inch (20 cm) pan with removable bottom.
2. Using a fork, mash 4 bananas with lime juice. Reserve.
3. Beat the butter and sugar until foamy.
4. Stir in egg, mashed bananas and coffee.
5. Spread mixture evenly in pan.
6. Whip the whipping cream and spread it into the bananas.
7. Distribute remaining cookies on top of the whipped cream.
8. Put in the refrigerator at least one hour.
9. Carefully unmold onto a serving dish.
10. Add lime juice to the remaining banana and arrange on Brazilia.

DESSERT

7th heaven chocolate and banana pie

Servings:
8 servings

Ingredients:

1 cup (250 ml) black chocolate chips 70% cocoa

4 Tbsp. (60 ml) coffee liquor or cocoa liquor

1 tsp. (5 ml) vanilla extract

1 12 oz. pkg. (349 g) silken tofu

1 Tbsp. (15 ml) honey

2 bananas cut length wise

Directions:

1. Arrange pieces of bananas on a pie plate so they cover the bottom and sides completely.

2. Melt the chocolate in a double boiler over warm water.

3. Remove from the heat source when the chocolate is almost melted.

4. Add the cocoa liquor and continue stirring with a spatula until the chocolate is smooth.

5. Combine the vanilla to the chocolate mixture.

6. Mix the tofu, honey and the mixture of melted chocolate in a blender until the mixture is silky smooth, about 30 seconds.

7. Pour this mixture over the bananas and refrigerate at least 2 hours.

8. Will keep in the refrigerator for a few days.

WARNING: the tofu must be soft type (silken tofu). Other types of tofu are not recommended.

OPTION: without the banana "crust", this pie makes a decadent chocolate mousse.

DESSERT

Unordinary chocolate and banana bread

Servings:
one bread or 8 servings

Ingredients:

1 ¼ cup (300 ml) sifted flour

1 tsp. (5 ml) baking powder

¼ cup (60 ml) unsweetened cocoa powder

½ cup (125 ml) unsweetened applesauce

½ cup (125 ml) brown sugar

2 eggs

3 ripe bananas mashed

1 tsp. (5 ml) vanilla extract

½ cup (125 ml) sour cream

¾ cup (180 ml) semi-sweet chocolate chips

Directions:

1. Preheat oven to 350 °F or 180 °C. Spray a 9 x 5 x 3-inch non-stick bread pan.

2. In a medium bowl, combine the first 3 ingredients.

3. In a separate bowl, beat the applesauce and brown sugar with an electric mixer at medium-high speed for 2 minutes.

4. Stir in the eggs one at a time. Mix well between each egg, scraping the edges if necessary.

5. Add bananas and vanilla mixing at a lower speed until it is well mixed.

6. Add the banana mixture to the dry ingredients alternating with the cream to the wet mixture. Mix with a large spoon.

7. Add the chocolate chips and mix it a few seconds.

8. Pour the mixture into the bread pan, and smooth the top.

9. Bake 55 to 60-minute or until a toothpick inserted in the centre comes out dry.

10. Let cool on a rack for 15 minutes, and then remove the bread from the pan to finish cooling on rack.

DESSERT

Chocolate and banana royal cake

Servings:
8 servings

Ingredients:

4 eggs

¼ cup (60 ml) sugar

1 cup (250 ml) flour, sifted

1 Tbsp. (15 ml) baker powder

1 tsp. (5 ml) cocoa powder

3 bananas mashed and mixed with a little lemon juice to prevent blackening

1 tsp. (5 ml) homemade chocolate syrup *

½ cup (125 ml) walnuts crushed

Directions:

1. Preheat oven to 350° F or 180° C.
2. In a large bowl beat the eggs with an electric mixer.
3. Add the sugar gradually stirring between each addition.
4. Mix the flour, baking powder and cocoa in another bowl.
5. Add the flour mixture alternating with the bananas in the egg mixture.
6. Add the chocolate syrup and nuts.
7. Pour into a Bundt pan which has been oiled and floured.
8. Cook for about 35 minutes. Cool on a rack.
9. Decorate with chocolate spread or frosting for brownies (next recipe).

* **CHOCOLATE SYRUP**: Mix 2 ml of sugar with 2 ml of water and 3 ml of cocoa powder.

DESSERT

Incredible raw chocolate banana brownies

The brownie was invented at the world exhibition in Chicago in 1893 to celebrate the 400th anniversary of the discovery of the new world by Christopher Columbus. Its name comes from its brown color.

Servings:
16 brownies

Ingredients:

BASIC INGREDIENTS

2 cups (500 ml) pitted dates

2 cups (500 ml) pecans or walnuts coarsely crushed

A pinch of sea salt

A pinch of orange zest finely chopped

2 tsp. (10 ml) vanilla

1 avocado ripe and mashed

½ cup (125 ml) cocoa powder

FROSTING

2 avocados and 1 small banana (ripe and mashed)

A pinch of sea salt

½ cup (125 ml) cocoa powder

½ cup (125 ml) agave or honey

Directions:

1. Put the dates in a saucepan, add 1 cup of boiling water and cover for 30 minutes. Remove excess water and crush the dates with a fork to make a paste.
2. In a food processor, combine all basic ingredients.
3. Pour into an 8 inch square pan (20 cm) and flatten the mixture.
4. In the same food processor, puree all the frosting ingredients.
5. Spread the frosting on the base of the brownies.
6. Cover with plastic wrap and store in the refrigerator at least three hours.
7. Cut into 2 inch square (5 cm) and serve cold.
8. Will stay fresh for two days in the fridge when covered with plastic wrap.

Chef's note:

Keep this dish longer by preparing it in a freezer friendly container. Cut the servings before storing in freezer. It will stay fresh up to a month in the freezer. Thaw about 45 minutes before serving.

DESSERT

Chocolate and caramelized banana empanadas

Servings:
20 to 24 empanadas.

Ingredients:
2 Tbsp. (30 ml) butter

2 Tbsp. (30 ml) brown sugar

A pinch of ginger and ground cinnamon

1 large ripe banana sliced

4 store bought flaky pie crusts, thawed

1 cup (250 ml) milk chocolate chips

⅓ cup (80 ml) finely chopped walnuts (optional)

1 large egg, beaten

ALCOHOL VERSION: use white rum instead of water for the egg mixture.

Directions:
1. Preheat oven to 375 °F (190 °C). Line a large baking sheet with parchment paper.
2. Melt the butter and brown sugar in a skillet over a medium-low heat.
3. Add the banana and spices and cook for 5 minutes, stirring constantly.
4. Remove from the heat and mash the banana with a fork.
5. Stir in the chocolate chips and nuts.
6. Place the pie crusts on a lightly floured surface. Using a 4 inch (10 cm) diameter cup or cookie cutter, cut out rounds.
7. Place the discs on the baking sheet. Place in the centre of each disc equal mixture of chocolate banana mixture leaving a half-inch (1 cm) edge.
8. Whisk egg with 1 Tbsp. (15 ml) of water. Brush egg mixture onto the edges of dough. Fold to enclose filling and pinch with a fork to seal. Brush the tops of the empanadas with the egg mixture. Bake for 20 minutes or until a golden color.

Chef's note:
To test the ideal amount of banana chocolate mixture to put in each empanada, make one at a time and adjust amount accordingly.

Beauty

Chocolate and banana scrub 57

Chocolate and banana body butter 59

Chocolate bath bombs 61

BEAUTY

Chocolate and banana scrub

Servings:
one treatment

Ingredients:
3 Tbsp. (45 ml) brown sugar

2 drops of almond oil or canola oil

1 tsp. (5 ml) cocoa powder

1 tsp. (5 ml) honey

One drop of banana extract

Three drops of chocolate extract

Directions:
1. Place all ingredients in a small bowl.
2. Mix by hand or with a spoon.
3. Massage the mixture on wet feet in slow circular movements by paying attention to the rough areas such as heels.
4. For more in-depth exfoliation, use a massage glove.
5. After the pedicure, apply Chocolate and banana body butter (next recipe) on your feet and let penetrate.

OPTION: you can use this scrub on other parts of the body, just double the quantities.

BEAUTY

Chocolate and banana body butter

Servings:
one cup

Ingredients:

1 cup (250 ml) coconut oil

1 Tbsp. (15 ml) white chocolate chips

½ tsp. (2.5 ml) chocolate liquor (optional)

Vitamin E (open three vitamin E capsules)

1 Tbsp. (15 ml) banana extract

1 tsp. (5 ml) vanilla extract

1 Tbsp. (15 ml) distilled water

Directions:

1. Melt coconut oil and chocolate chip on low heat in a double boiler over warm water.

2. Remove from the heat.

3. Add the remaining ingredients to the oil mixture.

4. Mix at high speed with electric mixer until the butter is creamy, about two minutes.

5. Transfer the butter to travel jars of 15 ml (available in pharmacy with self-adhesive labels included). Close with lids.

TIP: shake the mixture during the cooling time as cocoa will tend to descend to the bottom.

Keeps indefinitely in the refrigerator.

You have sensitive skin? Test on the inside of an arm.

BEAUTY

Chocolate bath bombs

Servings:
8 small bombs in cupcake shape

Ingredients:
1 cup (250 ml) baking soda

1 cup (250 ml) citric acid (available at natural food stores or where soaps are made)

½ cup (125 ml) cornstarch

½ cup (125 ml) light oil such as sweet almond oil

2 tsp. (10 ml) cocoa powder

3 drops of red or green food colouring

Muffins pans and cupcake liners

Directions:
1. Combine the first 4 ingredients to form a ball.
2. Separate the ball into two parts: one-quarter of the ball on one side and three quarters of the ball on the other.
3. Add cocoa to the largest ball and food colouring to the smaller ball.
4. Incorporate the color in each ball. (see below tip for this step)
5. Separate the largest ball into 4 parts and fill muffins liners.
6. Distribute the rest of the dough on top of the cupcakes to form the glaze.
7. Allow bombs to cure for a week at room temperature.
8. Remove them from cupcake liners after 48 hours.

WARNING CITRIC ACID: avoid contact with eyes and skin. Wear disposable plastic gloves and a mask for prolonged contact. Do not inhale the dust when you open the bag.

TIP: to avoid staining your hands with food colouring, pour dough into a plastic bag. Add the dye. Close and knead until the colour of the dough is uniform. You can also wear disposable plastic gloves when kneading.

HOW TO USE IT? Use one bomb in a bath filled with warm water. The sparkling lasts a few seconds. Will keep indefinitely if stored in a closed container at room temperature. Approximate cost per cupcake bomb: 50 cents

Chef's Notes